I0149190

An Introduction to Mindful Meditation

Adam Harbinson

Sarah Grace
Publishing
Dyslexic Friendly

Copyright © Adam Harbinson 2026
First published in 2026 by Sarah Grace Publishing
an imprint of Malcolm Down Publishing
www.sarahgracepublishing.co.uk

29 28 27 26 25   7 6 5 4 3 2 1

The right of Adam Harbinson to be identified as the author
of this work has been asserted by him in accordance
with the Copyright, Designs and Patents Act 1988.

All rights reserved. No part of this publication may be reproduced,
stored in a retrieval system, or transmitted in any other form or
by any means, electronic, mechanical, photocopying, recording
or otherwise, without the prior permission of the publisher.

British Library Cataloguing in Publication Data
A catalogue record for this book is available from the British Library.

ISBN 978-1-917455-35-0

Scripture quotations marked 'NLT' are taken from the *Holy Bible*,
New Living Translation, copyright © 1996, 2004, 2015 by Tyndale
House Foundation. Used by permission of Tyndale House Publishers,
Inc., Carol Stream, Illinois 60188, USA. All rights reserved.

Scripture quotations marked 'NIV' are taken from the Holy Bible,
New International Version (Anglicised edition). Copyright © 1979,
1984, 2011 Biblica. Used by permission of Hodder & Stoughton Ltd,
an Hachette UK company.
All rights reserved.
'NIV' is a registered trademark of Biblica. UK trademark number
1448790.

Scripture quotations marked 'NKJV' are taken from the Holy Bible,
New King James Version®. Copyright © 1982 by Thomas Nelson.
Used by permission. All rights reserved.

Cover design by Esther Kotecha
Art direction by Sarah Grace

Printed in the UK

Text divider designed by Freepik

Contents

Introduction to Mindful Meditation

If you don't change direction, you
might end up where you're heading.

(Lao Tzu, Chinese Philosopher born 571 BCE)

The aim of this book is to help its readers to find
peace and tranquillity in a frenetic and chaotic world.
But how do we achieve this state of inner peace? By
the regular practice of meditation. Meditation trains
our minds in the art of Mindfulness so that Mindful
awareness, living in the moment, will become a way of
life. We live in two places that don't exist – the future
and the past – but life is now. It is a simple practice,
but it is not easy.

Mindfulness can teach us how to deal with our
addiction to thinking, and help us find that quiet
place, deep within, where there is peace. Many

thousands of empirical studies since the 1970s have demonstrated that regular meditation can have significant mental and physical health benefits.

As we work our way through this 'guidebook' we will find how, with a little self-discipline, we can learn that while we cannot avoid stressful situations, Mindful Meditation can equip us to deal with stress in a quiet and thoughtful way, and by doing so we will begin to sleep better, it can lower our blood pressure and strengthen our immune system. Our relationship with friends and family will improve as it boosts our level of happiness, self-control and contentment.

In short, it works. Regular practice, even for only minutes at a time, several times a day can clear the clutter from our minds, it can quieten the constant chatter in our heads, still the torrent of thoughts that drown out our ability to see and hear and think clearly, and thus enable us to fully experience the beauty of the world in which we live.

We all seek happiness, but we will never find it if we persist on looking for it outside of ourselves. Isn't it ironic that while happiness is our natural state, and it is, we shall discover the absurdity of trying to find the happiness we seek by looking for it where it can never be found – outside of ourselves?

To illustrate this, there's a story of a man who had planned to take his family out to dinner. As he prepared to leave the family home there was a power cut, an outage, and in the melee that followed he dropped his car keys. He groped around in the dark in a futile effort to find them, and when he could not find them in the dark, he noticed that the street lamp just outside his house was lit, so he went near to it and continued his frantic search.

A neighbour noticed his plight and offered to help him. 'Where do you think you dropped your keys?' the neighbour asked.

'I think inside the house, but there are no lights in there, which is why I am searching here, under the light of the street lamp.'

Incomprehensible? Of course, but to be seeking happiness outside of ourselves is similarly futile.

Consider this: take a glass of water, shake it all about until it resembles a stormy sea, then notice that when you stop shaking it, it quickly becomes calm again. There is no need to exert pressure to still the water; it returns to its natural state, tranquil and at peace. Similarly, our natural state is one of tranquillity and peace, and regular practice of meditation will help us to understand that we already have the peace we seek.

Anthony de Mello (1931–1987) was an Indian Jesuit priest, a psychotherapist and spiritual teacher. He tells the story of a time when God grew weary of the constant stream of people always praying, always pleading for this or that, tugging at him, endlessly seeking his attention. So, God consulted with the angels: 'Where can I find respite? Is there not a place of solitude in my creation?'

Some of the angels suggested the dark side of the moon, others thought solitude might be found in the depths of the deepest ocean. But still the people came, until the Archangel Michael said, 'Hide yourself deep in the heart of man. He never goes there.'

A fanciful tale to be sure, but with an element of truth, for the angel was right. Deep in the heart of man there is a reservoir of stillness, where peace and happiness can be found, just as promised by our Lord when he said, 'I am leaving you with a gift – peace of mind and heart' (John 14:27 NLT).

Like the ocean, tumultuous waves might be thrashing about on the surface, but down in the deep, all is quiet and serene. The regular practice of Mindful Meditation can enable us to find that place of quiet serenity, regardless of our external circumstances.

Isn't it unfortunate that the last place we look for the peace and happiness for which we yearn, is in the depths of our troubled hearts? We think if we could own more of this, or had less of that, a bigger house, a chunkier bank balance, a more compatible partner, or none, then we would be happy. However, there is only one prerequisite: we cannot experience true happiness unless and until we have a peaceful heart. And that's what meditation can help us find.

Thomas R. Kelly (1893–1941), a prominent Quaker of his day, described the peaceful heart. He believed that deep within each of us there is an amazing inner sanctuary of the soul, a holy place, a divine centre, adding that it is a speaking voice to which we can keep returning.[1]

The ancient prophet Isaiah knew something about Mindfulness too, for in 750 BCE he wrote, 'In quietness and in confidence is your strength' (Isaiah 30:15 NLT).

Let's commit to finding that quietness and confidence together.

---

1. https://mypastoralponderings.com (accessed June 2025).

What Is Mindfulness?

Dr Mark Williams is Professor Emeritus of Clinical Psychology and Honorary Senior Research Fellow at the University of Oxford Department of Psychiatry. He and Dr Danny Penman, a writer and qualified meditation teacher, co-authored the ground-breaking book *Mindfulness: A Practical Guide to Finding Peace in a Frantic World*. Mark Williams defines Mindfulness as 'knowing directly what is going on inside and outside ourselves, moment by moment'.

Jon Kabat-Zinn is the creator of the Stress Reduction Clinic and the Center for Mindfulness in Medicine at the University of Massachusetts Medical School. He is seen by many as the father of Mindfulness, having been a practitioner for over half a century. He defines Mindfulness as simply paying attention, on purpose, in the present moment, without making judgements as if your life depends on it. And of course, it does.

That sounds simple, so let's break it down:

Paying attention: How often have you been engaged in conversation, and you realise that you're looking past your colleague? You are there but your mind, your awareness is elsewhere. Or you are walking by the shore, the birds are singing, the sun is shining, a soft breeze rustles the leaves and the waves lap gently on the shingle, but you have not seen or heard a thing, or, more correctly, you have not been paying attention, your thoughts are far away. Have you ever driven ten or more miles, and when you reach your destination, you have no recollection as to how you got there? You were driving on autopilot.

Mindfulness trains our minds to pay attention to the present, by being deliberately aware of what we are thinking. We become watchers of our thoughts and emotions.

On purpose: This suggests that whatever we are doing, or watching, or listening to, requires focused concentration. Paying attention is a deliberate act of seeing, feeling or hearing. Later in this book we will find numerous examples of exercises that will help us train our minds to live deliberately, to make every moment count. For example, we'll be considering ways in which we can consciously eat a raisin, or wash dishes, or simply walk, exercises that can surprise us as they enhance our life, and that by applying its principles we can come to know the power of a purposeful life.

In the present moment: Thich Nhat Hanh (1926–2022) was a Buddhist monk and peace activist. In his book *The Miracle of Mindfulness* he talks about washing dishes to wash dishes. I can relate to that, for often when I wash dishes I see it as a chore, an interruption to my after-dinner experience. But by washing dishes to wash dishes, by giving focused attention to the activity by being in the moment, I have found that washing dishes can be a pleasurable thing to do. You are aware of the soft warm feeling of the soapy water running over your hands and through your fingers. You will see the spectrum of colours in the bubbles, and you will concentrate on washing the dishes until they are clean. You wash dishes to wash dishes.

And finally, **without making judgements:** In other words, when you see something and you look deeply at it, or when you hear something, you listen deeply to it, you are aware of it. You don't analyse it or judge it by comparing it to past experiences, you simply see it, or hear it for what it is. It is what later in the book we will call the Beginner's Mind.

Another name for Mindfulness, given by Anthony de Mello, is 'Awareness'. Ellen Langer, Professor of Psychology at Harvard University, simplifies it further by calling it 'Noticing'. Being Mindful, Aware or Noticing means that when we walk in the countryside, we notice the trees and the clouds, we hear the birdsong and the crickets or the cicadas, and it is more meaningful than a cursory seeing and hearing.

Thich Nhat Hanh describes it as seeing deeply, hearing deeply, a practice that can dramatically improve your world in general, and your relationships in particular. For example, how often in a conversation do you find that instead of listening, you are waiting for the other person or people to pause for a breath so that you can jump in with your contribution to the debate, to which you have not really been paying attention? Practise listening deeply and the art of conversation will flourish and will become immensely more engaging.

Edward de Bono, in his book *How to Have a Beautiful Mind*, relates a scenario in which a beautiful girl and an old man were two of the guests at a dinner party. As the evening wore on, numerous guests approached the attractive lady, chatted for a couple of minutes and drifted off, and she was alone again. But the old man, described by de Bono as bald, with thick glasses and a pot-belly, was continually surrounded by people who wanted to be in his company. What was the difference? The lady wanted to talk about her life and her achievements; the old man was more interested to hear about the life experiences, the passions, the hopes and dreams of others. He was listening deeply.

What Mark Williams, Anthony De Mello and Thich Nhat Hanh agree on is that whatever we are doing, whether washing dishes, eating a raisin, walking by the sea or in a busy town, reading a book or engaged in conversation with another, being aware of what we are doing makes it real, alive and meaningful.

A Zen monk was asked, 'What do Zen Buddhists do?'

He answered, 'We walk, we sit, we eat.'

'We all walk, sit and eat,' replied the questioner. 'What's the difference?'

And the monk smiled and answered, 'When we walk, we know we are walking; when we sit, we know we are sitting; and when we eat, we know we are eating.'

A young novice monk was due to be interviewed by his superior as part of the progress of his career development, if that's not an unfortunate expression. As he was leaving his room he saw that it was raining, so he took his umbrella with him. Arriving at the temple he folded the umbrella and left it at the door.

'I see it's raining,' commented the Zen monk.

'Yes, it is,' said the novice.

'Did you bring an umbrella?'

'Yes, I did. I left it outside by the door.'

'Did you leave it at the right-hand side of the door or the left-hand side?'

'I don't know,' said the young man.

'Well then, come back next year,' said the Zen monk.

Now, that is Mindfulness on steroids.

Jon Kabat-Zinn has a way of bringing the experience of Mindfulness down to earth. For example, he suggests, 'When you enter the shower, check that you are in the shower.'

'Of course I am in the shower!' you might retort, but are you? Yes, your body is in the shower, but where is your mind? The likelihood is that your mind, your awareness, is anywhere and everywhere but in the shower. This simple suggestion is important, for by observing it regularly you are engaging in the process of training your mind to follow the example of the Zen monk: 'When we are in the shower, we know we are in the shower.'

Philosopher and spiritual teacher Jiddu Krishnamurti (1895–1986) adds a further layer of meaning when he says, 'The ability to observe without evaluating is the highest form of intelligence.' What I think he means is that we must train our minds to see things as if we have never seen them before. We tend to look at a tree and say, 'There is a tree,' but while recognising it as a tree, by labelling it, we evaluate it, we compare it to other trees we have seen, and from there we no longer see the tree as a unique creation. It's just a tree.

But look deeply at the tree, see it for what it is, touch it, feel its sturdiness, observe the contours of the gnarled bark, the shape and balance of the limbs to the left and the right, to the front and the back, the array of colours of the leaves if there are any, depending on the time of year. See its uniqueness.

Or when you stand by the shore, don't merely look at the waves as they lap on the shingle or sand, but look deeply, as if you have never seen such a phenomenon before. Notice the waves as they ebb and flow, how they advance and then try to retreat as the next one approaches. See how they create little eddies and whirlpools, how they flood the rock pools.

Mindfulness affords us the ability to see without judgement, without relating the object of your attention to previous experiences. Suddenly, everything becomes new.

Observe the shapes and contours on the face of the moon. Look deeply and your observation could be a revelation: the craters, the hills and valleys. Notice them, just as when you listen to a piece of music you dissect it, you identify each instrument, perceiving how they overlap and complement each other.

That is Mindfulness, Awareness, Noticing. Practise it daily and you will be amazed at how it enriches and enlarges your life, how it encourages you to slow down, to still your mind. You will very soon find that quiet, serene place, deep within, that has always been there but that you have been too busy, too preoccupied to engage with.

However, it is important to know that there is nothing new in the practice of meditation and Mindfulness. It is not a New Age trendy fad, even though in recent decades it has become something of a buzzword. Just one example for now: almost three thousand years ago the prophet Isaiah wrote, 'Forget the former things; do not dwell on the past. See, I am doing a new thing! Now it springs up; do you not perceive it? I am making a way in the wilderness and streams in the wasteland' (Isaiah 43:18-19 NIV). The implication being that if we are living in our past glories, difficulties or failures, we will not be equipped to see the wonders of what is taking place in front of our eyes, in the wonderful now. And of course, as Isaiah is encouraging us not to live in the past, two thousand years ago it was Jesus who said in the Sermon on the Mount, 'So don't worry about tomorrow, for tomorrow will bring its own worries. Today's trouble is enough for today' (Matthew 6:34 NLT). That's a prompt for us to avoid living in the future.

Look at Your Watch

Let's do a little experiment to demonstrate just how unaware we tend to be. If you are wearing a wristwatch, remove it and place it somewhere face down. Ask yourself the following questions: what colour is the strap? What colour is the face, and does it have a brand name on it? If so, where? Are there roman numerals, standard numbers, ticks or dots? Does it have a second hand? A date?

If you were able to answer all those questions correctly that is very unusual, and yet most of us look at our watches perhaps 30 or 40 times a day. That's in the region of 15,000 times a year you have looked at your wristwatch without really seeing it. And you know that there are times when we look at our watch, and if twenty seconds later someone asks what the time is we have to look again. The time of day didn't register with us. Our eyes were looking at the watch but where was our mind?

Create a Space For 'You'

Mark Williams gives us an example of how small things can make a major difference. One of his students related how as she walked from her car to her office each morning, she found herself really paying attention as her feet touched the ground, the feel of the fresh air on her face and in her hair, the fragrance of the flowers and the vegetation after rain. She told him how it became for her a little space where she could nourish herself in preparation for the day ahead.

She went on to say how it changed the entire day for her. She arrived at her desk feeling refreshed, with her mind still and quietened. She even began parking the car a little farther away thinking, 'This is really nice,' rather than frantically searching for a parking space that might save her a twenty-metre walk. By training her mind to pause, to live in the moment, she became the observer of her thoughts, no longer at the mercy of a tsunami of thinking that makes so many of us weary and up-tight even before our working day begins.

Make Time to Eat

Another example of how the practice of Mindfulness can enrich our lives mentally and physically is mindful eating. Take a moment the next time you are in a restaurant, observe how the people around you tend to cram food mindlessly into their mouths, often cramming more in even before they have properly processed what is already in their mouths. They are talking, or glued to their mobile/cell phone or reading, doing anything other than concentrating on what can be a wonderful experience, totally unaware of the layers of tastes and smells and textures. And their bodies don't benefit efficiently from the nourishment either, for it is by the deliberate and focused chewing of the food that enzymes are released in our saliva that aid with the process of digestion.

In one study, thirty healthy women consumed meals at different paces.[2] The women who ate more slowly consumed significantly less food, yet they reported

---

2. Study reported on the website www.healthline.com (accessed 28th June 2025).

that they felt fuller than those who ate more quickly. There's another possible benefit: weight loss.

Tara Parker-Pope writes a regular column in the New York Times under the title 'The Eat Well Challenge'. She regularly encourages her readers to take a few moments before starting to eat to contemplate everything and everyone involved in the process of bringing the meal to the table. Think of those who prepared the ground and planted the seeds, who fertilised and harvested the crops that became the ingredients, the drivers of the trucks who brought the produce to the market, the van drivers who transported it from the market to the shop, the shopkeepers, the storing of the food, the cooking, the presentation on the table.

See the veritable army of hard-working and dedicated people that is required to put that meal in front of you, then, slowly, begin to eat. Take small bites and you will taste the food perhaps as never before when your mouth isn't full. Chew the food carefully, deliberately and thoughtfully, noticing the tastes and colours, the aromas and textures of the food rather than gulping it down while engaging in conversation or watching TV. Try setting your eating utensils down between each bite, and the process of eating becomes more than a meaningful experience − it is much more nourishing.

Whatever we do, whether walking, showering, washing dishes, eating or talking with friends and loved ones, the more aware we train ourselves to be, the more meaning and enjoyment we extract from our activities. That is what meditation can do for us.

Eat a Raisin

Mark Williams, in his book *Mindfulness: A Practical Guide to Finding Peace in a Frantic World*, takes the simple example of eating a raisin to make a valid point, and I would encourage you to do this now if you can. Firstly, take a handful of raisins, pop them into your mouth and eat them as you would normally do.

Now try this . . .

Find a place where you can be alone and undisturbed for ten minutes, and please, lose the mobile/cell phone. Now, look closely at the raisin as you hold it in the palm of your hand, then roll it between your finger and thumb. Feel its textures, look at the raisin, observe how, as you gently squeeze it, it moves and changes shape.

Look deeply at the raisin, like you have never seen anything like it before, for when you think about it, you probably haven't ever taken time to notice its folds and wrinkles, the glossy parts and the dark crevices and ridges. So pause, and do this for a few moments.

Now place it in your mouth, and without chewing it, roll it around with your tongue, feeling the texture and any tastes that appear. Begin to bite into it, and slowly, without swallowing it, just be aware of what is happening in your mouth. Notice the explosion of juices as you continue to softly and thoughtfully chew the raisin. Notice how you are salivating (you are probably salivating now as you read this – I am as I write it). And now when you're ready, swallow it, paying close attention to the tastes and the after effects.

Have you ever been so conscious of how such a simple process as eating a raisin can be transformed, simply by paying attention? The taste, the fragrance, the feeling of the textures, firstly in your hand and between your fingers, then in your mouth, totally missed as you have stuffed handfuls of raisins or peanuts into your mouth? Now, imagine the effect of applying the exercise across all of your eating experiences.

Expand this activity of conscious awareness further when you next sit with a loved one or someone you know well and have spent much time with. Look deeply at them: deliberately notice the colour of their eyes, their eyelashes, their eyebrows, the texture of their skin, and their hair. Look at their hands, their fingers and their fingernails. You might be surprised at how much you have missed, just like the experiment with the raisin and your wristwatch. And so it is with life. Socrates is reported to have said, 'The unobserved life is not worth living.'

So What is Meditation?

Most of us live in two places that don't exist – the past and the future – from which we pay occasional visits to the present. Eckhart Tolle reminds us that we tend to live in a non-existent past or an imagined future. And Richard Rohr agrees. He believes that the mind can only reprocess the past, judge the present and worry about the future. But we can train our minds to live in the present moment – the only reality that exists – paying occasional visits to the past or the future. However, we will find that our minds do not like the present.

Meditation is about training our minds to live in, to experience and to enjoy the present, the naked now. But how? Many people try to meditate by emptying their minds, getting rid of thoughts, but however hard you try to do this, you will find it impossible to rid your mind of thoughts for more than a few seconds.

Meditation is not about emptying the mind.

When I began meditating over two decades ago, I imagined in my mind's eye a big blackboard with nothing written on it. Every time a thought entered my mind, it appeared as handwriting on the board, and I set about erasing it. But I was spending more time erasing the thoughts than doing what I wanted to do. I wanted to rest. I wanted the incessant activity of my frenetic mind to stop, but my mind had a rebellious mind of its own.

I invite you now to take a minute to think of nothing, no thoughts. But to demonstrate how little control we have over our thinking, you must not think about a pink polar bear.

Well, how did you do? Not very well, I imagine. And what about the pink polar bear? If you were able to eradicate it from your thinking, that is rare indeed. No, meditating is not about emptying your mind. If so, you could bang your head against a wall or find a way to induce a coma; that just might empty your mind, but that is not meditation. Meditation is to be aware of your surroundings, aware of your body: warm, cold, afraid, relaxed, at peace or in turmoil. It's about noticing. You notice your thoughts, you become the observer of them as they drift into your mind and then, like a cloud sailing across a clear sky, they drift away again. In meditating you simply let them pass by.

Think of it this way: thoughts are like people walking past your open door; you can see them and you can hear them, but you don't have to follow them, you don't get involved with them.

We shall do a number of exercises as we work our way through the book, but I invite you now to notice something very simple. Whatever you are doing, make yourself aware of some sensory perception. It could be the sound of the wind or the hum of a fridge, a dripping tap or traffic outside your window, or the sensation of your feet touching the floor. Just be aware of the sensation . . .

Did you notice that as you focused on that sensation, however briefly, your thinking momentarily stopped? The addiction was paused just for a moment. As you begin to practise meditation you will notice that even after just a few seconds your mind will begin to wander again. However, before too long, by regular practice you will find that those few seconds of 'not thinking' will expand, enabling you to dip down into that place of quiet serenity that Thomas R. Kelly speaks about. But don't be discouraged; it's normal for the mind to wander, even for people who have been meditating for years. Indeed, the fact that you became aware that your mind was wandering is good. That is meditation.

Let's Do a One-Minute Meditation

Find a place and a time where you are unlikely to be disturbed. Silence the mobile/cell phone, just for a minute. Sit comfortably, feet flat on the floor, eyes gently closed or lower your gaze in an unfocused way, and soften the muscles on your face with a half-smile. Sit upright, back not supported by a chair if you can, with your hands resting softly on your lap.

Be aware of your surroundings, notice the feeling of your feet in contact with the floor, the sense of touch as your hands rest one on top of the other on your lap. The important thing is to relax. I would advise not to set a timer, for you will probably be distracted by the thought, 'Is it about to go off soon?'

Now breathe a deep soft breath, inhale ... exhale . . . just be aware of your breathing, your lower body rising as the air is drawn into your lungs. Notice the coolness of the air as you inhale, and then as you exhale be aware of its warmth as it passes through your nose or mouth.

Don't force your breathing. Your lungs have been breathing unaided from the moment your umbilical cord was cut, just be aware. Remember that when your mind wanders, you are not failing, you are noticing that your mind is wandering. Meditation is all about training your mind to be an observer of your thoughts rather than being subject to them, driven by them. But your mind can be like a wild stallion, some call it a monkey mind that will not easily comply. Your mind has a mind of its own. It doesn't like the present; its default position is the past or the future, ruminating or imagining, but regular meditation trains your mind to be more still, more focused, and more at rest in the present.

If in this minute your mind wanders, as it will, notice where it has wandered to, and then gently return it to the awareness of your breathing, but do it with self-compassion. Imagine your thoughts as items on a conveyor belt; they appear, drift across your line of vision for a few seconds and then they are gone. Don't follow them.

Be encouraged. If you return your awareness to your breathing a hundred times, that's like doing a hundred press-ups in the gym. You are training your mind as you train your body. Just as if we go to the gym to get physically fit, we don't do one press-up and expect an enviable physique – it takes time. So it is with meditation, you are training your mind.

Try one breath without your mind wandering . . . Good, now another, and another. That's progress. You might find it helpful to imagine you are in a cinema, watching as your thoughts are being projected onto the screen in front of you. You are observing, but you don't allow yourself to get involved.

Now gently open your eyes and breathe a deep and easy breath as you end this exercise. If that was your first experience of meditation, take a moment to explore how you felt and how you now feel. If you feel relaxed and energised, allow yourself to be excited. If not, don't be disappointed, for you are taking baby steps in a process that can enrich and enhance every aspect of your life, mentally and physically. All the evidence emerging from thousands of studies confirms that regular meditation can improve your physical and mental health.

However, regardless of how much you develop the practice of meditation, it will not remove stressful situations from your life, but you will learn how better to handle stress.

Mindfulness is not meditation, meditation is not Mindfulness, but they are inextricably linked.

Mindfulness is a way of life, a chosen lifestyle; meditation trains our mind to be Mindful, to be aware, to notice our surroundings, to be conscious of our thoughts, our sensory perceptions of sound and sight, of smell and touch, to be aware of them in the moment, for as we will repeat over and again, this moment, this 'right now' is all we have of life. We are not living next week, nor are we living last week, now is all we have. Let's explore that.

I think of the words of Jesus in the Sermon on the Mount, the 'distilled wisdom of the ages'. He demonstrated his understanding of the profound link between Mindfulness and deep inner peace when he said, 'That is why I tell you not to worry about everyday life – whether you have enough food and drink, or enough clothes to wear. Isn't life more than food, and your body more than clothing? Look at the birds. They don't plant or harvest or store food in barns, for your heavenly Father feeds them. And aren't you far more valuable to him than they are?' (Matthew 6:25-26 NLT).

In other words, don't focus your mind on the future, live in the present and know the perfect freedom of now.

The Power of Now

To the extent that we live in two places that don't exist – the past and the future – our lives are characterised by anxiety, fear, stress and depression. Thich Nhat Hahn puts it simply; he says that the future is an image. It is not reality. The past is an image, neither is it reality. The only reality is now. Our entire lives are now.

One of the world's leading spiritual teachers, Eckhart Tolle, confirms this when he says that we never do, feel or experience anything that is outside the present moment.

Isn't it the case that we tend to live in regret or fear of the past? We allow it to cast its dark shadow over what might otherwise be a bright and peaceful present. We focus on things we did that we wish we had not done, or things we did not do that we wish we had.

Or there will be times when we wish we were back in those halcyon days of warm summers and long carefree evenings rather than the unpleasant now. Oli Doyle, in his book *Mindfulness for Life*, observes that dwelling on the past leads to anger, regret, sadness and grief. Think about that. Is he right?

But we can also find ourselves living in the future, wishing that we could escape to there from our present life of drudgery and disappointment, unhappiness and failed relationships, unfulfilling careers or poor health.

Or we might be living in dread of the future: 'My partner might leave me ... My business might collapse ... My children might not achieve what I want and expect for them ... My health might fail,' and all the while the beauty of our 'now' passes us by unseen. Oli Doyle's view of the future is that dwelling on the future can cause stress, anxiety, worry and fear. I know that to be true.

I remember being really stressed when my late wife was terminally ill, but looking back over the years I can now see that my grief was perhaps compounded by past regrets and my anxiety and fear of a future alone. If I had been able to focus more on the present and less on the past and the future, my grief might have been easier to bear, and I might have been better positioned to help and support my critically ill wife. Mark Twain once said, 'I am an old man and have known a great many troubles, but most of them never happened.'

In Anthony de Mello's book *Walking on Water*, he tells of one of his patients who was paralysed as a result of an automobile accident. Startlingly the man told him that he really began to live after he was left paralysed. For the first time in his life, he had time to look at himself, time to see, to really observe his life, his reactions and his thoughts. His life became much deeper, richer and more meaningful than before.

Look Back,
But Don't Stare

Mindfulness can teach us that it is normal to look back, but without staring. We recognise the lessons life has taught us, we can plan for the future but always remembering that the past and the future are images, they are not reality. The only reality is now.

I lead a class of about fifteen adults who meet regularly to practise meditating and to share our experiences. We are a group of ordinary people, male and female, mostly retired or semi-retired, people who have grown tired of being pushed around, dictated to by life. Often, after only a very few sessions, new members report that they are sleeping better, they are more at ease with themselves, more energetic, less judgemental. Things that used to frustrate and bother them, like bad driving and annoying neighbours, they now shrug off with the view that in the grand scheme of things, 'Is this really important?'

Their lives are calmer and they soon find the peace that has eluded them for so long. It's good to be at ease with ourselves, but isn't it a shame that it is often not until later in life that we find the place of quiet tranquillity that we thought we could enjoy only if we owned more, or had this situation or that difficulty in our lives resolved.

Three Challenging Questions

However, it is never too late to change. I was in my sixties before an emotional crisis forced me to ask the question, 'Does it have to be like this?' and I discovered that there is a better way. Richard Rohr, Franciscan priest and founder of Center for Action and Contemplation based in New Mexico, helps here by posing three challenging questions – questions that I often ask myself: 'What is my life like?' 'What should it be like?' and 'If I am not content with it, what am I going to do about it?'

Many people agree on the wisdom of writing a letter to their older self, telling what sort of person they plan to be in ten or fifteen years' time in as much detail as you can. Try it now. Do you want to be in the same job as they are in now? Look at your friends, do you want to grow older in their company? What habits do you want to nurture or be rid of in your older, wiser self? Do you want to be on a healthier diet? Do you still want to be smoking?

Those are three challenging questions with a potential to bring about real change: what do you like about your life, what do you not like about it, and what are you going to do about it? In summary, what I'm suggesting is this: decide what sort of person you want to be in ten or more years' time, and then write yourself a letter, telling yourself what you are aiming to do to ensure that you will be the person you want to be when you reach that age, starting right now. That is living deliberately.

The practice of Mindfulness can enable us to find answers to those questions. It can put us in the driving seat where we belong, no longer a passenger in our own lives, no longer drifting, no longer allowing ourselves to be dictated to by the vagaries of life. However, they must be our own answers, not the ambitions or expectations of another, neither guru nor a self-designated spiritual guide, but based on our own personal and unique inner knowing. Motivational speaker Earl Nightingale taught, 'You are in charge of your life to the degree that you are in charge of your thoughts.'[3]

Few of us have a clear picture of what our lives are like or where we are going, still less of what life should be, or could be like. How much do we know of the

---

3. https://www.azquotes.com/author/10824-Earl_Nightingale (accessed 11th July 2025).

immeasurable creative potential we possess? Often our default position is that we crash and reel daily from crisis to crisis, like a half-drowning man in a wild river, only just managing to keep his head above water, and sometimes not. Far less do we take time to try to figure out that there might be a better way.

How many of us can relate to the story of a man on a galloping horse? A bystander shouts, 'Where are you going?' and the man on the horse answers, 'I don't know, ask the horse!'

It's not unusual to hear someone say that they do not have time to sit for three or four minutes each day meditating, no time to pause, no time to reflect. But by building the practice of meditation into our daily routine we will find that we will be more creative, more original in our thinking, and because we can become more effective in all aspects of our daily life, we will have more time to ourselves, not less.

In this regard I think of Blaise Pascal who said, 'All of humanity's problems stem from man's inability to sit quietly in a room alone.'[4] Thought by many to be an overstatement, but he does have a point.

As we become more creative, we will find that rather than not having time to pause and meditate, we will be better equipped to embrace life's difficulties, and as a result we will have more time to do what we

---

4. https://www.goodreads.com/quotes/19682-all-of-humanity-s-problems-stem-from-man-s-inability-to-sit (accessed 12th August 2025).

want to do, what we need to do, and in doing so we will find that our lives are lives of enjoyment and excitement, not drudgery.

Creative or Angry?

It is not possible to be angry and creative at the same time. As we shall see later, the emotion of anger originates in a small part of the brain known as the amygdala, and when the amygdala is fired into operation, it overrules the prefrontal cortex, the brain's thinking and rational function.

For now, let's picture this scenario: you are driving to the airport, you allowed sufficient time for the journey but the traffic is moving too slowly for your liking. You come to a set of traffic lights that are red and you have the choice of pulling up behind a car in either lane, and you choose to pull up behind a single car in the right-hand lane (if you are in a country where you drive on the left). There you sit, impatiently waiting for the lights to turn green, fingers drumming on the steering wheel, and when the lights turn green the car in front signals to turn right, so you are forced to wait there until the oncoming traffic clears. You could have chosen the inside lane, the one that is now proceeding effortlessly into the distance.

What do you do? You have a choice, and therein is the key. You can choose to blast your horn, clench your fists on the steering wheel, shout (audibly or inaudibly) at the stupid person, the bad driver in front of you, the cause of your being late for your early morning flight. Your face turns red, your heart pounds and the veins stand out on your neck . . . or you can take a big easy breath, aware that all your tantrums and fuming will not change anything except your blood pressure. You choose to wait, calmly wait.

Read through that paragraph again. Focus on the contrast: fury, raging blood pressure, red face, anger, pounding heart, or you take a big easy breath, you choose to wait. You might say that you can't help it, it's the way you've always been, but I have quoted this scenario to many people, and almost without exception they say that they have found that it cannot be done. But many come back to say that having tried, they have broken free from their 'autopilot'. The takeaway here is that you have a choice.

Own the Thought, But Don't Act On It

However, let's not pretend. Such a scenario I find infuriating. To pretend that my natural reaction is always to relax with a deep easy breath and a half-smile in the face of such provocation is fantasy. It is simply not the case, and to allege that all is calm within all the time just doesn't ring true. But a lady in one of the Mindfulness classes I lead taught me a valuable lesson. She offered a means of resolving the potential flash point with the words, 'Own the thought, but don't act on it.' I might one day get to the place that Thich Nhat Hahn occupied, always at peace, but for now I'm happy that I don't routinely act on my initial stimuli. I guess I'm happy to admit that I am a work in progress.

We will read later something I have spoken about and written about many times, Viktor Frankl's space: a practice that can change your life. And I can assure you that if you try it, even just once, you will begin to plumb the depths of the peace and serenity that resides deep inside each of us.

Remember Thomas R. Kelly's description of that inner sanctuary of the soul, the holy place, the divine centre? Look at the choppy sea, waves churning it into 'white horses' on the surface, and yet however wild it is on the surface, down at the seabed all is quiet. That deep inner peace is always there, and we can find it, beginning now, but we must want to.

And there is yet another benefit associated with the daily practice of meditation and Mindfulness. The experience of most people is that as they grow older, time appears to pass more quickly, but by practising Mindfulness you will find quite the opposite. Days that once were crammed with frenzied activity now amble by at a relatively more leisurely pace, for we will be more relaxed than ever before, even though our family demands and business and social problems are unlikely to have dissolved away.

Busy is the New Stupid

In a conversation between Bill Gates and Warren Buffet – two of the wealthiest men on the planet, aged 69 and 94 respectively as I write in 2025 – they compared diaries. Bill's was crammed, every day packed with back-to-back meetings while Warren's had wide open spaces every day. It appeared to have impacted Bill Gates to the extent that his conclusion was, 'Busy is the new stupid!'

Think again of the half-drowning man in a wild river, only just managing to keep his head above the raging current. Mindfulness teaches that we can climb out of the river to stand on its bank to observe the mayhem from which we are now detached. The river is still there, but now you are in control of your thoughts, rather than being dictated to by life's events. Remember Earl Nightingale: 'We are in control of our lives to the degree that we are in control of our thoughts.'

Read and ponder on what Eckhart Tolle has said:
'Your life is not determined by what happens to you,
but by how you respond to what happens, and how
you respond to what happens to you, determines your
future.' Now, pause, reflect and ask yourself, is it true?
Dr Gabor Maté echoes Tolle when he says, 'Trauma is
not what happens to you, it's what happens inside you.'

We have seen that another word for Mindfulness
is 'Awareness'. For example, when we are washing
dishes, we can be aware that we are washing dishes.
When we sit, eat or walk, we know we are sitting,
eating or walking. Mindfulness enables us to train
our minds to live in the moment, so that even a
dull experience such as washing dishes can take
on a whole new meaning. When we are driving,
Mindfulness can enable us to be aware that we are
driving, to be aware that we are eating when we are
eating.

I visit the city of Glasgow frequently, and on a
recent trip I made a conscious decision to look up,
to notice the beauty of the early nineteenth-century
architecture of that great Scottish city. So much
had I missed on my hundreds of previous visits. The
invigorating power of living in the moment can make
even the mundane activities in which we are engaged
enthralling.

Think again of Mark Williams' student who walked mindfully from her parked car to her office each morning, refreshing herself for the day ahead, so much enjoying the experience of walking deliberately, feeling the soft thud as her heel made contact with the ground, the cool air on her face and in her hair, that she began to park her car farther away. And yet the default position of so many of us is to rush and panic and get stressed and uptight because someone has taken our usual parking space. And what state are we in when we finally arrive behind our desk? Frazzled, gasping for a coffee to help us calm down, and already incapable of grappling effectively with the demands of the day?

Another simple exercise is when we walk about in our homes, moving from one room to another. Try pausing to observe the door handle, to hear the creak of hinges, or the sound of a loose floorboard underfoot. And when travelling through our home town, we can deliberately raise our eyes to observe the beautiful architecture to which we are too often completely oblivious.

When we take a walk in the garden or in a local park, a familiar place, we can deliberately make ourselves aware of the contours and shapes and colours of the shrubs and flowers, or the trees, the song of the birds, the refreshing fragrance of the vegetation after rain, and the splash and gurgling of the stream as it tumbles its way to the sea. We will be amazed at the beauty that is all around us, the explosion of colours and shapes that have escaped our attention. This is living!

Later we will consider a research project conducted by Professor Richard J. Davidson, founder and chair of the Center for Healthy Minds at the University of Wisconsin. In the study Professor Davidson provides verifiable evidence that, on average, we are not aware of our surroundings for almost half of our waking lives.

Think about that, and think about what we are missing: the sound of the wind in the trees, a smile on the face of a friend, a family member or a neighbour, or a piece of calming music. That piece of scientific research tells us that for almost half of our lives we are not there. 'We're not there to know we're not there,' notes Professor Ellen Langer in her inimitable style. But where are we? We are lost in the future or locked in the past – two places that don't exist – and we are missing the vibrancy of life, lost in images that we think are reality.

At a recent seminar the speaker asked, 'Where is your mind?' Most people tapped the side of their heads in response, but no, the experience of most of us is that our minds are all over the place. Richard Rohr says that our minds resemble a Mexican jumping bean. For example, if you have read from the start of this book you will agree that if you were to start again, you would see things that you had no idea that you had just read.

Alone in a Crowded Hall

Picture the scene: a man went with his wife and young daughter to the theatre to see a performance of Tchaikovsky's *The Nutcracker Suite*. They found their allocated seats deep in the heart of London's Royal Albert Hall. They were just a little late, climbing over people to get to their allocated seats; some were tutting in annoyance at the latecomers. But just as the conductor's baton began directing the musicians, the man realised he had left the keys in his new car.

All the way through the spell-binding performance, he thought of nothing but his shiny new car. It might be stolen or vandalised, or valuable contents stolen. And what was the result of his uncontrolled thoughts? He saw and heard nothing of Tchaikovsky's *The Nutcracker Suite*. Similar to Jon Kabat-Zinn's suggestion, when you're in the shower, make sure that's where you are. This man was in the Royal Albert Hall but, in reality, that was the last place on earth he was. Understandable perhaps, but how silly. What could all his frantic worrying do to protect his car? Nothing! But doesn't it sound familiar?

It is similar to James Joyce's observation in his book *Dubliners*: 'Duffy lived a short distance from his body.'

Too often we are like the child in a play park, screaming with delight while playing on a roundabout, but looking across the park at another piece of entertaining equipment. The child leaves the roundabout and runs to the slide, but now he is watching a little boy playing on the swings. He can enjoy neither the slide, the swing nor the roundabout.

Mark Williams again: Mindfulness is paying attention, on purpose, in the present moment, without making judgements. Simple? Yes, but not easy, for our minds have minds of their own.

A Practical Example

Can you relate to this scenario? You're sitting on a park bench by the sea or in a leafy park. You've just had a disagreement with your partner, and you have gone outdoors to cool down. Your head is buzzing: 'Why did I say that? Why doesn't s/he understand me? What's going to happen to this relationship? If we part, who's going to pay the mortgage, and what about the children?' You become angry – angry with yourself and angry with your partner. Your heart pounds, every muscle in your body quivers with tension and you can see no solution to the situation, and the circumstances surrounding it go around and around in your head.

Now stop for a moment! Just stop!

Relax your clenched fists and your gritted teeth. Release the tension in your stomach by taking a series of big easy breaths. Soften your face with a half-smile and bring your awareness to the feeling of the cool air passing through your nose. Feel your abdomen rising as the air fills your lungs, and your warmed breath as it leaves your body. Don't force your breathing – your body knows how to breathe – simply relax and be aware of your body breathing.

Your mind will wander back to the current source of stress, of course it will, that's natural, it's what minds do. Your mind will insist on returning to the argument you have just had but adds nothing to it by way of reconciliation. And then it will jump to the future, imagining the outcome of your disagreement. Then it will jump to the past again in an effort to find the origin of the disagreement. Yes, of course your mind is wandering, but the difference now is that you are aware that your mind is wandering. That's your 'Aha' moment, and it's a major step forward. Your mind will dredge up every argument you have ever had, linking them where it is unlikely that there is even a tenuous link, apportioning blame and counter blame, but now you can take control, take a step back, choose to be an observer of your thoughts rather than remain at their mercy.

The source of your anger has not dissipated, but now you are calm, or at least you are calmer. Now you can take a step back, you can observe the situation objectively. You can transform your anger into creativity by dealing with the situation rather than wasting your energy on your emotional roller coaster. Anger, reason and creativity are mutually exclusive.

By practising Mindfulness you will quickly discover for yourself what I have said a number of times: your mind has a mind of its own, and it does not like the present. It seems to be at home rummaging about in the non-existent past, or dreaming in the imagined future. But rather than allowing yourself to be tossed around like a rag doll by your anger and your fears, your hopes and dreams, you have taken a step back, you have become an observer of your thoughts. You are the watcher, detached from your thoughts and are therefore much more capable of dealing objectively and creatively with challenging situations.

It is liberating when we realise that we don't have to slavishly follow every thought that happens to drop into our minds, leading us on a merry dance. We are not our thoughts. Thoughts are mental events, and like clouds scudding across an azure sky, they drift across your line of vision and then they are gone, if you allow them. They are like people walking past your open window: you can see them and you can hear them, but you don't have to follow them.

Practise observing your thoughts, take a back seat in the cinema of your mind. You are not involved in the turmoil on the screen and, as a result, you will be able to locate and engage with your peaceful heart. But where does this peace come from? It has been there all along, peace is our natural state. When you train your mind to live in the present moment, your consciousness will find the inner peace, that inner sanctuary of your soul, the peace promised by Jesus: 'I am leaving you with a gift – peace of mind and heart' (John 14:27 NLT).

Another Exercise

Jon Kabat-Zinn describes meditation as 'dropping into your body'. Dr Ellen Langer prefers to use the expression 'bringing body and mind together'. As we have already seen, Kabat-Zinn says that when we take a shower, make sure you're in the shower. Of course we're in the shower when we're in the shower, but are we? Sure, our body is in the shower, but our mind is who knows where. Mindful Meditation brings body and mind together.

So, as with the one-minute meditation we did earlier, let's do a three-minute guided meditation now. Find a comfortable seated position in a place where you are unlikely to be disturbed, preferably on a straight-backed chair so that your spine is self-supporting if you can, with your feet flat on the floor, your hands lying loosely on your lap. Your eyes can be open, looking in an unfocused way at the ground just in front of your feet, or softly closed, whichever is most comfortable.

Sit quietly for half a minute or so, just to arrive, making yourself aware of the sensations surrounding you in the room, maybe a refrigerator humming or street sounds from outside. If you hear a passing car or a train, the song of a bird or the wind in the trees, it's important not to try to ignore them. Just be aware of them, note them, but don't follow the thoughts, wondering what type of bird is singing or where the car or train is going to. Just be aware of the sounds.

Now, bring your awareness to the feeling of your feet inside your footwear, or the firm feeling of your contact with the floor, wiggle your toes, relax your feet and ankles. If there is pain or discomfort, don't focus on it, just be aware of it. Moving your awareness up your body, be aware of any tension in your calves, your knees, then your thighs, your abdomen, your neck and shoulders. Slowly and with self-awareness, soften and relax your face with a half-smile.

Bring your awareness to your breath, breathing normally, feel your chest rising and falling, your abdomen moving out and in, the coldness of the air as it enters your nostrils and the warmth as it leaves through your mouth or nose. Your mind will wander, but that's OK. Remember that thoughts are like items on a conveyor belt: they appear, move across your line of vision, and disappear. You don't have to follow them or wonder where they have gone.

It is a very human thing to think that if your mind is wandering you will never be able to meditate, but I don't mind repeating, even experienced meditators freely admit they struggle with their monkey mind. I have been practising meditation for a couple of decades and still have difficulty at times. When I do, my focus is not to try to ignore the thoughts that drift into my mind; I simply am aware of them, I note them, and I can do that. I choose not to follow them.

I will meditate by focusing on just one breath, then another, one breath at a time, and it's not unusual for me to have difficulty getting beyond six breaths. Then I start again, one breath at a time. So, be encouraged – the fact that you are aware that your mind has wandered is exactly what meditation is about; you are aware.

Simply and with self-compassion, note where your mind has drifted to, and then bring your awareness back to your breath. Don't give yourself a hard time, be patient with yourself.

Remember, as we have already said, if your mind wanders a hundred times, and you return your awareness back to your breath a hundred times, that's training for your mind, the same as your hundred press-ups in the gym is part of training your body. The mind will always wander but, very soon, after a month or so you will find that your wandering mind is wandering much less frequently. Actually, it's probably not; the difference is that now you become aware of your restless mind much more quickly. That's progress, as a result of your regular meditation you are training your mind.

Now sit still for a couple of minutes, focusing on your breathing, aware of sounds and movements in and around the room, returning your awareness to your breathing over and over again as often as is needed as your mind flits back and forth. If you find it difficult or frustrating, go easy on yourself. As I have suggested, try it for one breath, then two, and then perhaps for a minute, and when you can do that, success! For if you can still your mind for just one minute you can do it for two minutes, and thus you build your practice of regularly meditating.

Now that is a simple example of meditation. Take a note of how it felt living in the stillness of the present moment. Relaxing? Freeing? However, if you do that even just a couple of times a day for a number of weeks or months you are likely to find those very positive feelings becoming more and more imprinted on your lifestyle. I have found it more beneficial to start each day with a time of such meditation, it sets me up for the day. You too will find your life will become more mindful, more at peace and more grounded. You will be less vulnerable. And you don't need to sit in a lotus position to meditate. For example, if you are driving, pause, check where your mind is, notice any stiffness in your body, your knees or your shoulders, and just for a few minutes, bring body and mind together. Jon Kabat-Zinn again: drop into your body.

Mindfulness enables you to live in the moment, aware of what you are engaged in, just like the Zen monk who was asked what do Zen Buddhists do: 'When we walk, we know we are walking; when we sit, we know we are sitting; when we eat, we know we are eating.'

With the regular practice of meditation, before long you will find that when you become aware that your body is here but your mind is elsewhere, almost instinctively you will take a big slow easy breath, bringing body and mind back together. Taking charge of your mind is the first step in taking control of your life.

Here's a practical example of an early unexpected benefit of mindful living I experienced. The last day of an eight-week course I once took part in was a day of silent retreat. Our tutor encouraged us to spend the day as a day of 'Mindful Meditation'. Quietly we walked barefoot around the grounds of the beautiful Clandeboye Estate on the outskirts of Bangor in North Down where I live. My closest companion on that course was a big South African rugby coach called Charlie, a gentle giant.

As the ten of us returned to the room where we were based, suddenly Charlie burst out, 'I've got it! I've got it!' He had discovered that when provoked or stimulated to react to an event, we have a choice. We don't have to react thoughtlessly as we always have while living in the autopilot mode, behaving and reacting as we always have, simply because we always have. We can pause, take just a second to think, and then choose how to react.

We will learn more about this strategic pause later, but this was a profound discovery for Charlie, and the rest of the class too, for what Charlie had discovered was what Victor Frankl wrote about in his book *Man's Search for Meaning*. Frankl (1905–1997) was an Austrian neurologist, a psychiatrist and a Holocaust survivor who became prominent following his liberation from Auschwitz. We shall look more deeply into Viktor Frankl's 'space' later.

At that time, I lived in a cottage in the village of Crawfordsburn in North Down where I had a dedicated parking space for my car. Occasionally when I arrived home, usually late in the evening, someone had parked in my space. Furious, I would go indoors, power up my computer and printer and write: 'WHAT PART OF "NO PARKING" DO YOU NOT UNDERSTAND?' and plaster it all over the offending car's windscreen.

A few days after Charlie's discovery I arrived home as usual at around 11 o'clock one evening, and there was a car in my space, but this time my first thought was, 'I'll park somewhere else.' And it wasn't until an hour or so later it dawned on me: Hey, this is working!

I could have reacted in a number of ways. I could have fumed and raged as I normally did, or I could have felt the same frustration, but while owning the thought I could have chosen not to act on it. The third way is to act as I did that evening, and that is evidence of neuroplasticity, the brain rewiring itself through the regular practice of meditation. I was beginning to experience that what we practise grows stronger, as proposed by Professor Shauna Shapiro. We'll meet with her later too.

You Are Not
Your Thoughts

Picture yourself in a raging river with the mad current sweeping you along in its path. You are fighting the force of the river but to no avail. Most of us know that life can be like that at times. Max Lucado, American author and public speaker, tells the story of a parrot, sitting serenely in the tranquillity of his cage one day when the lady of the house was dusting and vacuuming her home. She noticed the untidy mess at the bottom of Polly's cage. Gingerly she opened the little door and stuck the nozzle of the vacuum in to suck up the detritus, the droppings and discarded feathers, but she unbalanced as she stood on a stool, lost control of the nozzle, and the poor bird disappeared into the body of the machine.

Quickly she dismantled the vacuum, retrieved her pet bird and set about washing him by ramming him under a jet of cold running water, then dried him with a blast of hot air from her hair drier before reinstating him on his perch with a glazed look on his face.

'Polly doesn't talk much these days,' she explained to a visitor. 'He just sits there, staring vacantly into space.' I'm sure most of us can relate to Polly the frazzled parrot.

However, Mindfulness can enable us to extract ourselves from the frenzied and uncontrolled activities of our mind, in the same way that climbing out of the river to stand on the bank can rescue us from its raging current, to watch the river, unaffected and free. If we feel afraid, or anxious, it is important to acknowledge, perhaps audibly if it is appropriate, that you *feel* afraid or anxious, but you are not afraid, you are not anxious.

Imagine for a moment that there has appeared the possibility of a threat to your financial position. You cannot rest, you cannot focus on your tasks in hand. Imagine that as you try without success to get your thoughts straight, someone you love (maybe a grandchild), suddenly and without warning bursts into your room. You hug the child, the fear goes, the anxiety melts away, perhaps only temporarily, but for now your thoughts of disappointment and fear of loss have dissipated. You might be subject to your thoughts, but you do not have to be. You are not your thoughts; you are the observer of your thoughts.

Meditation enables us to train our minds to distance ourselves from our thoughts so that, regardless of the turmoil that rages without, we can be at peace. By the regular practice of meditation, we are discovering a fundamental truth that will enable us to be free to enjoy the stress-free life for which we have always longed.

We are not our thoughts.

Eckhart Tolle, in his book *The Power of Now*, tells how when he was almost thirty years old, he had lived with debilitating depression for most of his adult life. One morning he felt worse than usual as he lay in his bed trying to find the motivation to drag himself into the new day. He describes how a deep longing for annihilation, for non-existence, was beginning to overwhelm the instinctive will to live, and in desperation he uttered the words that radically changed his life: 'I cannot live with myself any longer.'

As he repeated those words over and over, a peculiar thought took root in his mind, 'Am I one or two? If I cannot live with myself, there must be two of me: the "I" and the "me" with whom "I" cannot live. Could only one of them be real?'

He describes how he was stunned by the thought, his mind whirled and when he became aware of his surroundings, for the first time he heard the chirping of a bird outside his window. 'If a diamond could sing,' he thought, 'that's the sound it would make.' Tears filled his eyes as he walked around his room, recognising it as his room but aware that he had never really seen it before, and he marvelled at the beauty and aliveness of it all.

Mindfulness can do that for us; it has done it for me. I have travelled the world quite widely but it is only since I began to practise Mindfulness that I have become aware that the stretch of coastline not a mile from my home is such a beautiful place, I would not wish to be anywhere else. I see the swirl of colour and shapes on the wing of a tiny butterfly. I would pause conversation with the company I was with and together we would watch a tiny field mouse playing on a blade of grass.

On more than one occasion I have become aware that as I had walked along a familiar part of the path my mind was elsewhere, and I was able to retrieve my awareness to witness the shape of a tree I had not noticed before, although I had travelled that way perhaps hundreds of times. I would find myself walking by the shore and realise that for some minutes I had not seen or heard anything of the outstanding beauty that lay before me. And there have even been times when I have retraced my steps, deliberately seeing and hearing the unique beauty of my world that I had just walked past, my mind being who knows where. Meditation can train us to live Mindfully in the wonderful freedom of the present.

Mindfulness is an awareness of the world around us, but it is more than that: it is an awareness of who we are and of our place in the world. It is an awareness of our emotions and feelings, an awareness of how an appreciation of our environment can enrich our lives, and that to appreciate anything, we must be aware of it. And as we continue to practise this Mindfulness, this awareness, we will learn to listen deeply to people we love as we communicate together. Perhaps they will not be saying anything new, maybe even droning on about the day at the office, or the inclement weather, but we will hear them as we have never heard them before, and we will see them in a new light, for we will be looking and listening deeply as never before.

Less and less will we be careering through our brief days, needlessly lost in worries and fears, the scudding clouds and crashing waves, the whispering trees and the beauty of the wayside flower, even the little field mouse playing on a blade of grass will speak to us of the majesty of nature, the nature of God. We will begin to live. And do trust me, it's never too late to begin the practice of Mindfulness.

My sincere hope and prayer is that as you apply the simple principles I am introducing you to, that you too will discover the peace that is already embedded deep within you.

A Wandering Mind is an Unhappy Mind

Richard J. Davidson is professor of psychology and psychiatry at the University of Wisconsin-Madison and founder and chair of the Center for Healthy Minds. He tells of a research project he carried out and reported in the American magazine *Science* in November 2010 under the title 'A Wandering Mind is an Unhappy Mind', by Killingsworth and Gilbert, two Harvard psychologists.[5]

An App was developed that was designed to send text messages three or four times a day to a representative sample of people, 2,250 respondents from a range of occupations and ages. The text asked three questions:

- What are you doing right now?

- Are you thinking about something other than what you are currently doing?

---

5. https://www.instagram.com/reel/C-IUxEzBcOZ/ (accessed 10th August 2025).

- On a scale of 1 to 10, how happy are you right now?

The results were astonishing. Firstly, 47 per cent of the respondents reported that they were thinking about something other than what they were doing as the text pinged its presence. But more significantly, those who reported that they were concentrating on whatever it was that they were doing, registered a higher factor of happiness. And it didn't matter if the activity in which they were engaged was pleasant or unpleasant, interesting or boring. The researchers also concluded that mind wandering is the cause, not the consequence of unhappiness.

The lesson here is simple: if we want to be happy, we need to learn how to take charge of our minds, and this we can do but it takes practice. Think Earl Nightingale again: 'We are in control of our lives to the degree that we are in control of our thoughts.' We need to understand that we do not decide to think, we just think incessantly, addictively.

Now that we're approaching the end of this book and have had several forays into the practice of meditation, let's perform another exercise to check on our progress. We have established that it is normal for our minds to wander, and that when we decide to meditate, we can expect our thoughts to shoot about all over the place. That's a good starting point, for then we will find it easier to exercise self-compassion and patience towards ourselves, and that's important.

We have seen that when our minds wander and we return our awareness back to our breath a hundred times, we are doing a hundred press-ups in our mind-gym, and there is much scientific evidence supporting this view. By repeatedly returning our awareness to our breath, we are training our mind to notice more quickly when our mind wanders. That is the result of a phenomenon known as neuroplasticity, and we'll learn more about that a little later.

Now, the exercise, and this time I am proposing that you do it every day for a month. Once again find a comfortable position. Some practitioners insist on a straight-backed chair which I too recommend, for the practical reason that if you choose a big soft cushy seat, you're likely to drift off to sleep. Try not to lean back into the chair, but keep your spine straight if you can, self-supporting and relaxed with your feet flat on the floor. Close your eyes or lower your gaze in an unfocused way, soften your face with a half-smile and allow your hands to lie loosely on your lap.

Bring your attention to your breathing. Just be aware of the cool air passing through your nose as you inhale and the relative warmth of the air as you exhale, feel your abdomen rising and falling. Don't force your breathing, just be aware of it, but this time, try to pay particular attention to the pause between your breaths. Of course your mind will wander — by now you should know that's normal — but remember that the realisation that your mind is wandering is central to meditation. Don't allow yourself to get frustrated or impatient with yourself, don't yield to the temptation to think that you're wasting your time. Each time your mind wanders, you simply bring your awareness back to your breathing, patiently with self-compassion.

Now, the point of this exercise is that you do it regularly, every day for a month. You don't have to do it for an hour at a time, a few minutes are enough, perhaps several times a day, during those times in everyday life when you bring mind and body together, when you notice that you have become a little stressed, or you feel a tightness in your shoulders. The good news is that you don't have to sit in the lotus position.

It is more than likely that even just after a month or so you will notice a difference in your attitude to every aspect of your life; stressful situations just don't seem quite so stressful as they used to. You will relate to those around you, in the home or at work or college, more gently, with more patience and tolerance. You will have begun to train your mind and you will notice how much less your thoughts are tending to wander.

Neuroplasticity in Operation

The simple definition of neuroplasticity is this: it is the brain's ability to change as a result of experience and learning. Many thousands of experiments since the development of MRI scanning technology in the 1970s have confirmed that the brain is constantly being rewired. As early as the 1920s, psychologist Karl Lashley was conducting research on rhesus monkeys that he believed demonstrated changes in their neural pathways, which he believed was evidence of what we now recognise as neuroplasticity. But his work was not taken seriously by the establishment. The accepted view at that time was that once the brain is fully developed, usually in early adulthood, it was fixed and incapable of further change. Neuroscientists believed that neuroplasticity manifested only during childhood.

However, research in the latter half of the twentieth century, and increasingly in the last couple of decades, demonstrates that the brain is constantly changing, and that it has the potential to change well into old age, and it can change every day. That has significant implications for learning, memory and even recovery from traumatic brain damage. Neuroplasticity is the ability of the brain to form and reorganise its connections.

Think of the brain as a network of busy city streets: some are used frequently and the traffic moves quickly and easily. These roads represent our habitual ways of thinking, feeling and doing. The more often we travel along these roads, the more fluent our ways become. Sadly, we will often hear people say, 'Well, that's just the way I am and I have no intention of changing.'

When my oldest son was at medical school in Aberdeen on the east coast of Scotland, he introduced me to one of his colleagues, who is now one of Scotland's prominent psychiatrists. His name is John. In a conversation with John on one occasion I cynically asked him what psychiatrists actually do for people who have a mental health issue, and he explained, 'When I am with a patient, I will lead him along one of his familiar life's paths, and I'll ask, "So what do you routinely do when you arrive at a situation like this?" and the patient will answer, "I usually do this, or that."'

'Good,' John would say, 'but why don't we try a different approach?' It's analogous to turning right rather than the usual left. And so, by repeatedly turning left rather than what he habitually did by turning right, his usual well-worn pathways will soon become overgrown and the new neural pathways grow stronger. Like a frequently used city road, it becomes more fluent and is no longer a road less travelled. The patient's brain is beginning to be rewired.

Professor Shauna Shapiro has conducted numerous scientific experiments that produce empirical evidence supporting her hypothesis that what you practise grows stronger.[6] If you always respond to a situation in the same way, then those neural pathways grow stronger. It's called Cortical Thickening – a verifiable and visible change takes place in the physical structure of the brain. Regular practice of meditation trains the brain to be mindful, to be aware of our habitual reactions, our autopilot, or our familiar neural pathways, and so by being aware, we are no longer at the mercy of our entrenched mind.

I go to the gym two or three times a week and, being a creature of habit, I go into the changing rooms and turn right. I always turn right and select lockers 3, 5 or 7, depending on their availability. On a number of occasions I decided to challenge my autopilot by deliberately doing something different. So instead of entering the changing rooms and turning right to my usual choice of locker, I chose to turn left and used the first available locker. I was surprised at how uncomfortable it felt to do that, but it reinforced in

6. https://www.youtube.com/watch?v=IeblJdB2-Vo (accessed 13th August 2025).

my mind the extent to which we can become a slave to our autopilot.

Shapiro posits that as we challenge our old neural pathways, they become overgrown and 'what we practise grows stronger', by the process of Cortical Thickening.

Let's look at what can happen when we choose to question our response to life's situations.

Avoid the
Amygdala Hijack

The amygdala is an almond-shaped structure in our brain. There are two of them, one on either side, just above the ears. The name is derived from the Greek word meaning 'almond', and their primary role is to process our emotional responses. The amygdala is the emotional centre of the brain linking our emotions to many other brain activities, especially memories, learning and our sensory perceptions. When we are angry or afraid, the amygdala is triggered into an emergency response and immediately overrules the prefrontal cortex, preparing us for fight, flight or freeze. The prefrontal cortex is responsible for decision-making, reasoning, planning and social behaviour.

Here's how it works. The amygdala detects a threat from information it receives from our sensory perception, mainly our eyes and ears. Its job is to ask the question, 'Am I safe?' But it cannot distinguish between real threats and perceived threats. For example, you overhear an insulting or threatening comment in company directed at you. Or if you are addressing an audience and you see someone rolling their eyes, the amygdala's job is to trigger an immediate emotional response.

However, the problem is that the amygdala is not programmed to take time to analyse the perceived threat, and so the body is instantly primed to respond, in the same way as it would if the threat was a bear emerging from the woods and heading in your direction: racing heart, sweaty palms, tense muscles and raised blood pressure. It responds so quickly that the thinking, rational part of our brain – the prefrontal cortex – is frozen out. It doesn't have time to consider whether the threat is real or imagined, or even if a response is appropriate. It doesn't have time to ask such obvious questions as: 'Is it possible that the comment I have just heard was actually directed at me, or could it be that I have taken that comment out of context? Was that individual rolling their eyes because of something I said? And even if so, is it appropriate for me to deal with it just now?'

Or imagine a businessman running his company on a shoestring. He sits behind his desk and his phone rings. It's his bank manager telling him that his overdraft facility is being withdrawn. Danger is detected by the amygdala and, as instant panic ensues, he either falls into deep depression and fear or he becomes verbally violent; the reasoning part of his brain is switched off by the instant reaction of the amygdala. More often than not, by the time the prefrontal cortex engages with the situation, it's too late, you can't undo what is done or unsay what has been said, and you hear yourself say, 'Why on earth did I say those things?' What has happened?

You have suffered an amygdala hijack!

The trouble now is that your amygdala believes it has done a good job and thinks, I must do that again. Remember Shauna Shapiro? What you practise grows stronger? Many scientific studies using cutting-edge scanning technology indicate that when the amygdala frequently triggers our emotions, such as fear or anger, it actually increases in physical size, the result being that we react stressfully more often and more vigorously to situations that the amygdala perceives as threats. Similarly, many studies have provided empirical evidence that as my rugby-playing friend Big Charlie discovered, if we pause for a second or two before reacting, we are giving our prefrontal cortex an opportunity to choose how to react to the perceived threat in a reasoned and thoughtful way.

And so it is that with frequent and regular practice of meditation and thoughtful responses, the amygdala reduces in physical size, and therefore the response to stress triggers is significantly and noticeably reduced. We still experience stressful situations, but we deal with them more quickly, more efficiently and thoughtfully. But how do we avoid this hijack?

This is where Viktor Frankl's 'space' comes into its own. As soon as you detect your body reacting to the amygdala's stimulus, you pause, just for a few seconds, long enough for the prefrontal cortex – the rational and thinking part of your brain – to engage by asking, 'What emotion am I experiencing right now? What caused it? And why did that particular event cause that emotion?' Your pausing to consider these questions is evidence that now your thinking brain is overruling the amygdala and you thoughtfully and deliberately decide whether or not to respond, and, if so, how and when.

Viktor Frankl's Space

One of Viktor Frankl's most oft repeated quotations is: 'Between stimulus and response there is a space. In that space is our power to choose our response. In our response lies our growth and our freedom.'[7]

In an average day you can be sure that something unpleasant will take place, someone will say something to provoke you, you might be reminded by email of some negative happening in the world, or the weather might turn sour to ruin your summer barbecue. This is the stimulus.

The question is, what will your reaction be? It is reasonable to suggest that you will respond as you usually do, possibly by flying into a rage, or by becoming either verbally or physically abusive. But take a three-second pause, use that space to decide how you will respond, and you will find that in that response lies your growth. Why? Because you are

---

7. https://www.mindfullifeskills.com/blog/between-stimulus-and-response (accessed 31st July 2025).

taking charge of your thoughts, your reactions and, ultimately, your life.

Most of us desire personal growth, and we all desire freedom. But freedom from what? Freedom, I suggest, from the chains of 'how it has always been'. We get frustrated with ourselves when we react in the way we always have, saying things we wish we had not said, things that we know we cannot unsay. How tiresome it can be to hear others, even ourselves say, 'Well, that's just me. I've always been like that and I'm too old to change.' However, we are never too old to change, but we must want to.

Pause now, for just a moment. Remember an occasion when you reacted in your usual characteristic way, perhaps witnessing an incident of careless or dangerous driving, or an insult directed at your person. Later, how frustrated do you become, perhaps saying, 'Why do I always say or do that?' Now imagine the same scenario, only this time you pause, just for two or three seconds, take a breath, but this time you decide how you will respond to the familiar stimulus. How you respond is to an extent secondary. What really matters is that you choose how to respond. You take charge of your thoughts and reactions. Remember? You are in charge of your life to the degree that you are in charge of your thoughts.

Think of the example that I quoted earlier: you pull up behind a car at the traffic lights, ready for a speedy getaway, but when the traffic lights turn green the driver of the car in front switches on his indicator to turn right, or left, depending on which side of the road you are driving. You have a choice: you can rage and fume, or you can choose to pause, take a breath and relax, aware that there is nothing you can do to change the situation. Loosen your vice-like grip on the steering wheel, soften your face with a half-smile and, suddenly, all is peace rather than tension and another dose of killer stress.

What is happening here is that you are noticing the amygdala's stimulus, and you pause, just enough for the prefrontal cortex – the rational and thinking part of your brain – to engage and overrule the amygdala. That simple exercise has the power to change your life; it did mine.

Immeasurable Wealth

Mooji Baba, a Jamaican spiritual teacher, tells the story of two friends who grew up in the same village and who spent a lot of time together; they had total mutual trust. One day Pablo told his friend Miguel that he had a lot of money, but he did not want his wife to know about it. He was fearful she would spend it all, so he hid it under the floorboards of his house.

'I am planning to go on a long journey, Miguel,' he said one day, 'and I want you to know that I have hidden some money in my home. I want you to know where the money is, just in case I don't return.' And so he brought his friend to his home and showed him where the cache of coins were buried in a back bedroom. Then he set off on his journey, as it happened, never to return. Some years later Miguel was walking through the village where Pablo and he had grown up, when he saw Pablo's wife and children begging in the street.

'Why are you begging?' he asked them, and he was told that Pablo had passed away. He was heartbroken, but he told the little family that their father had left them a lot of money. 'Come, quickly, and I will show you.' And they made their way back to their home and watched with bated breath as Miguel began to remove some key floorboards. Sure enough, there was a treasure chest, filled with gold coins.

Now, the question is, were that mother and children a wealthy family? Yes, they were, even as they begged in the street, but they were totally unaware of their significant wealth. And that is how it is with many of us. We were born to achieve, to be creative, born with potential to be great, to be what we were destined to be. God wants the absolute best for each of us, but perhaps we have believed the lie told us by significant others: 'You are like your wayward father, you'll never amount to anything.'

One of the underlying principles of life was summed up over three thousand years ago by King Solomon, believed to be the wisest and wealthiest person who has ever lived. He wrote, 'As [a man] thinks in his heart, so is he' (Proverbs 23:7 NKJV).

We are what we think.

The Beginner's Mind

I am a newspaper columnist and have been for over a
quarter of a century. I consider it a privilege to have
my columns, on a wide range of subjects, published
in ten to twelve regional newspapers across Northern
Ireland. The following is a column I wrote shortly after
discovering the value of the 'beginner's mind' and
how to cultivate it. Although much could be written
about the subject, that's for another day perhaps, but
meanwhile I think it sums it up pretty well:

*I have to admit it, however often I say that today
is the first day of the rest of my life, there are
times when I find myself acquiescing to the
norms and expectations of society, blundering
through the day, with ghosts of the past or fears
and insecurities of the future lying heavy on my
stooped shoulders.*

*However, I have discovered an ancient system of
thought that inspires me, that enables me to see
myself as work in progress. The Buddhists call it*

'Shoshin'; *the Japanese word for the Beginner's Mind. Maybe it's what Jesus had in mind when he said, 'Unless you change and become like little children, you will never enter the kingdom of heaven' (Matthew 18:3 NIV).*

Through it we can recover the mind of a child, unsullied by the mists of time. I have eight grandchildren, five of whom I rarely see for they live in far-flung lands, but three of them live nearer home in Scotland, so I'm a frequent visitor to the land of thistle and bagpipes.

I treasure my trips to Greenock, walking along the Esplanade towards Gourock with little Phoebe or Lois or Simeon holding tightly onto my hand is priceless, eyes dancing when they see a grey seal, or a tern diving into the Clyde for its breakfast. The mind of a child is fresh and bright, their world is filled with awe, excitement and curiosity. They live in the moment. What you and I take for granted, to them is a wonderful novelty. The world has not yet transformed their joy and sense of wonder into the relative drudgery of adulthood. You know: 'I've seen it all before.'

My question as I write on this bright sunny morning is, does it have to be that way? Must the untarnished outlook of childhood be lost forever? No, it doesn't have to be that way, and yes, we can live again in the brave new world of perpetual discovery.

How? Take a thoughtful walk through a place as familiar as the town where you live, and pause. Imagine you have never been there before. Look at the faces of the people around you, take time to be aware and wonder at the architecture, hear the myriad sounds of the traffic that assail your senses. Notice the smells of food cooking in the restaurants, the birdsong and the rustle of the wind in the trees. There you will recover your Shoshin, *your beginner's mind. My daily prayer is, 'Lord, help me to see things I have never seen before, or things I have often seen, but in a new way.'*

We have a choice; we can remain locked in the daily grind of our own personal hamster wheel, or we can live with the receptive and teachable mind of a child, always observing familiar sights with fresh new eyes.

Marcel Proust, who penned the novel In Search of Lost Time, *understood this when he wrote, 'The real voyage of discovery consists not in seeking new landscapes, but in having new eyes.'*

Man, Know Thyself

We can be prone to self-deception at times. Not only do we want to present ourselves in the best possible light to our friends, our colleagues and our family, but we can choose to turn a blind eye to certain aspects of our own behaviour that we ourselves don't like to see. Particularly as we develop Mindfulness as our new way of life, we will notice the disparity at times between how we respond to challenging situations and how we know and wish we should. We expect ourselves to put into practice what we have learned when someone treats us in an unkind way or when life disappoints us, but often we are shocked when we react as if we knew nothing about Mindfulness.

I want to be open and honest with myself, but I find myself fuming on the inside, behind a plastic smile, or a smirk that I hope will mask my 'old man', so my Mindfulness practice doesn't always produce the results I want. Reflect on what we read of Viktor Frankl's space: 'Between stimulus and response there is a space. In that space is our power to choose our response. In our response lies our growth and our freedom.'

Now the point here is that we must not beat ourselves up because of that initial 'autopilot' urge to explode, for thus it might always be. But there is a positive here – we have grown, because now we are aware that we have a choice, now we can decide how we will respond. Remember the man on the galloping horse? 'Where are you going?' asked a bystander. 'I don't know, ask the horse.' No longer will we be careering through life, lurching and reeling from crisis to crisis. We can be in control.

Yes, we can surprise and disappoint ourselves by how we react to a negative stimulus, but we can maintain our integrity in such situations. As we have already learned, we can own the thought, acknowledge our reaction, but we do not have to act on it. Own your reaction to an unwelcome provocation, don't pretend to yourself or others that this surge of anger or frustration isn't there. It is, but take a Viktor Frankl step back, take advantage of the space, and then respond how you choose to respond rather than submitting to the dictates of your autopilot. Soon your amygdala gets the message: 'there's no room for stress here'.

The Prayer of Serenity

*'God, grant me the serenity to accept the things I
cannot change, the courage to change the things
I can, and the wisdom to know the difference,
living one day at a time, enjoying one moment
at a time, taking this world as it is, and not as I
would have it.'*

I want to end on a high; my take on the Prayer of
Serenity. Penned by, or attributed to, the American
theologian Reinhold Niebuhr (1892–1971) in 1943, but
it has its roots in the teachings of Epictetus, written
down and published for us by his pupil Arrian in the
second century CE and available today in a little book
entitled *Enchiridion*.

The word '*Enchiridion*' can be roughly translated
'handbook' and it was, and remains, fundamental
to the Stoic philosophy. The first page of the book
contains the following words, which you will agree is
echoed in Reinhold Niebuhr's interpretation that we
recognise today as the Prayer of Serenity:

Of things some are in our power, and others are not. In our power are opinion, desire, aversion, and in a word, whatever are in our own acts. Not in our power are the body, property, reputation, offices [magisterial power], and in a word, whatever are not our own acts.

He then goes on to say that if we confuse the two, trying to control what is beyond our power to control, *'you will lament, you will be disturbed, you will blame both gods and men: but if you think that only which is your own [to control] to be your own . . . no man will ever compel you, no man will hinder you . . . no man will harm you, you will have no enemy'.* In other words, you will live in freedom. And psychologists agree: the vast majority of mankind's stresses and anxieties are caused by trying to control what cannot be controlled.

After winning her match in the 2021 US Open quarter finals, the young outsider, 18-year-old tennis wonder-woman Emma Raducanu was asked, 'What is your secret? How can such a young and inexperienced player look so cool, so controlled on the court?' Emma was quoting a well-known mantra oft repeated by sport psychologists: 'Control the controllables, be in the moment, and concentrate on the next point.'[8] And the rest is history – three days later she went on to win the grand slam.

Emma Raducanu was right, and we would do well to emulate her advice: control the controllables, be in the

---

8. https://www.youtube.com/watch?v=DwWyZaUMhRs (accessed 20th June 2025).

moment, and concentrate on the next matter in hand. But we must distinguish between what is controllable and what is not. If Emma Raducanu had focused on trying to control her opponent – the uncontrollable – the outcome is likely to have been completely different, for as Epictetus reminds us, if we try to control what is beyond our power to control, we will lament, we will be disturbed, and we will blame both gods and men.

Our challenge is to know the difference between what we can control and what we cannot. And therein is our peace.

Final aphorism:

If you do not change direction, you might end up where you are heading.

(Lao Tzu, Chinese Philosopher born 571 BCE)

Bibliography

De Bono, Edward, *How to Have a Beautiful Mind (London:* Vermillion, 2004).

De Mello, Anthony, *The Way to Love* (New York: Image Books Doubleday, 1992).

De Mello, Anthony, *Walking on Water* (New York: Crossroad, 1998).

Doyle, Oli, *Mindfulness for Life: A Six-Week Guide to Inner Peace* (London: Orion Spring, 2015).

Epictetus, *Enchiridion* (Mockingbird Classics, 2017).

Frankl, Viktor, *Man's Search for Meaning* (Rider, 2011).

Hahn, Thich Nhat, *Living Buddha, Living Christ* (London: Rider, 1996).

Joyce, James, *Dubliner* (London: Grant Richards, 2014).

Krishnamurty, Jiddu, *The First and Last Freedom* (San Francisco: Harper, 1975).

Langer, Ellen, *Counter Clockwise* (London: Hodder & Stoughton, 2010).

Maté, Gabor with Daniel Maté, *The Myth of Normal* (London: Penguin, 2024).

Proust, Marcel, *In Search of Lost Time* (CreateSpace Independent Publishing Platform, 2015).

Rohr, Richard, *The Naked Now* (New York: Crossroad, 2013).

Tolle, Eckhart, *Stillness Speaks* (London: Hodder & Stoughton, 2003).

Williams, Mark and Danny Penman, *Mindfulness: A Practical Guide to Finding Peace in a Frantic World* (London: Piatkus, 2011).

www.ingramcontent.com/pod-product-compliance
Lightning Source LLC
LaVergne TN
LVHW051425080426
835508LV00022B/3243